Mapping the Borderlands
Haibun and Tanka Prose

Mapping the Borderlands © 2025 Barbara Sabol
Cover design: Tom Baldwin
Cover art: Katina Pastis Radwanski
Author photo: Michael Murray
ISBN: 978-1-962405-15-7

Sheila-Na-Gig Editions
Russell, KY
Hayley Mitchell Haugen, Editor
www.sheilanagigblog.com

Mapping the Borderlands

Haibun and Tanka Prose

Barbara Sabol

Sheila-Na-Gig Editions

Advance Praise for Mapping the Borderlands: Haibun and Tanka Prose

Sabol displays a wide variety of forms and subject matter to explore connections between human and animal life. Traditional haibun, juxtaposing prose and haiku, are deftly augmented with tanka and one-line haiku, while subjects include wild, domestic, dream, and zoo animals. With insight and wonder, she ponders a question made explicit in the concluding essay: whether humans can know their true nature without a close connection to the animal world. As her poems so eloquently testify, she believes we cannot.

—Barry George, author of *Sirens and Rain*

Quarry swims, cave walks, and gorge hikes are a few of the territories explored in *Mapping the Borderlands*. Barbara Sabol's haibun and tanka prose tenderly embrace the realm of "furry, finned, or winged otherness" and gently invite us to explore our inner landscapes of wilderness and wildness.

—Marilyn Ashbaugh, Editor, *Under the Bashō*

Barbara Sabol takes us on a journey where civilization meets the wild and "benevolent mysteries" occur—dolphins coming to the rescue, a beloved dog safe after three days missing, "the god of not-yet" bestowing luck—and where we witness the comfort of nature forever "cycling into what comes next."

—Cynthia Anderson, author of *The Far Mountain*

Sabol's poetic turns of phrase display her reverence for the flora and fauna of the world and all its "benevolent mysteries." With a vigorous sense of optimism, the poet wanders the immensity of a polar bear's dream and shares in the camaraderie of a pod of dolphins. Quiet and contemplative, Sabol offers her readers the tranquility and promise available to each of us when we commune with the "furry, finned or winged otherness" that abounds in every environment. *Mapping the Borderlands* is a beautiful, heartening book that makes me want to hit the trail. Explore.

—Peter Newton, editor of *Contemporary Haibun Online*

Acknowledgments

I wish to thank the editors of the journals in which the following poems were published, at times in an alternate format or with a different title:

Café Haiku: "Anticipation"
Contemporary Haibun Online: "Crossing the Threshold," "Jigsaw"
Drifting Sands Haibun: "Crosscurrent," "Endangered," "The Wildwood" (winner of the 2025 Rachel Sutcliffe Memorial Haiku-Arts Award)
Failed Haiku: "In Wait"
Frogpond: "Quarry"
Light Enters the Grove: Exploring the Cuyahoga Valley National Park Through Poetry: "Ode to Spring, Peeper"
Modern Haiku: "Why Our Mothers Warned Us About Playing in the Creek"
One Art: "In the Garden I Am Reminded," "Traveler"
Paloma Press website: "Nanuq," "Passing By"
Presence: A Journal of Catholic Poetry: "Letting the Kneeler Down"
Pudding Magazine: "Late Light"
Ribbons: "Messenger" (originally titled "Night, Porch")
SWWIM everyday: "Willingly"
The Ekphrastic Review: "In the Wound of Night"
Vita Poetica Journal:"Flare."

Gratitude also to the editors of the journals in which the following haiku were first published as individual poems:

Acorn: "glass lake"
Cattails: "perpetual whirl"

Haiku Netra: "the ceiling fan's"
Pages Literary: "immense heaven"
The Heron's Nest: "moon flower"

Special thanks to my writing partner and dear friend, Marion Starling Boyer, for her generous attention to these poems. The value of her critique and support is beyond measure. Gratitude also to fellow poets in the larger haiku community, and especially to the Ohio Haiku family for their teaching and fellowship through the years. Thank you to editor, Hayley Mitchell Haugen, for believing in this work and shepherding the poems into book form. It is quite the honor to have a second book published by Sheila-Na-Gig Editions. How special it is to have the fabulous painting, "Ascent," by my artist friend, Katina Pastis Radwanski, grace the cover of this book. As always, I am thankful for my husband, Tom Baldwin, for his bottomless belief in my work and his graphic art magic in the creation of the cover design. And hardly least, a deep bow to the creaturely realm, the animals that live among us, both as companions and wild wonders who embody the best of ourselves.

The owl and rabbit were wondering,
along with the trees, if the air would soon fill with snowflakes,
but the power that moves through the world and makes our
hair stand on end was keeping the answer to itself.

from "Sheep in the Winter Night"
—Tom Hennen

Fish twitched beneath me, quick and tame.
In their green zone, they sang my name.

from "Morning Swim"
—Maxime Kumin

Contents

Messenger

We gather on the porch, old friends, talking of things
of the day—Eileen's raspberry pie, the report of a new
species of sea star, how much else there is to discover.
And, of course, the weather. Cool this spring; a mercy
to the orchard keepers here in the valley.

Our voices hush as darkness falls, imperceptibly at first
until someone says, *Look! The Dipper.* Someone else,
The moon, there in the pond. We lean forward
in our chairs, attuned to bullfrogs' guttural calls,
cricketing in the mud-sweet grass. Rustling
in the woods beyond.

We let the candles burn down; our faces visible in a spill
of house light. Then, somewhere among the trees, coyotes
begin their plaintive chorus. Something in me rises up,
an urge to call back, an ache finding its voice. A barn owl
joins in. Its shriek almost human. We forget about pie crust
and the elements; silenced now in the great shadow
of the hidden world.

suspended
from the stone lintel
a clearing bell. . .
the white raven
pauses to listen

The Wild Wood

Mid-winter darkness is already falling as I trek through a foot of new snow, searching for my dog, Lumi. Venturing off-trail through the woods, I hold out my lantern, the only source of light this moonless night. The park ranger says, "Coyotes probably got her." I'd rather imagine that she has entered an enchanted kingdom where a rabbit, seeing that she is lost, snuggles her in its burrow or that she has found shelter in the bole of a tree.

hobo spider
i too
spin my web

This morning, a call from a hiker who spotted a dog matching Lumi's *missing dog* picture. I drive to the edge of the park, miles from where I lost her three days ago. Atop a steep hill that arches down to the river, I call her, long and loud, the way my mother would sing my name when the street lights came on. A form takes shape at the bottom of the hill—a snow swirl or my small, white dog? Rib-thin, mud-slushed, exhausted, she comes limping toward me. I scoop her up, cradle her under my jacket and together we bow to the benevolent mysteries that move through the forest.

second bloom
frost flowers
glaze the field

Chimera

Trick of the light, I think, when the seal's head crests in the water
of this small cove where I'm swimming. A distance of ten strokes.
Less. We keep that distance a long minute—me treading water, riveted.
The seal dips, rises, turns a dark eye toward me. Curious, but not enough
to come closer. On impulse I swim out to where he last dove. Just
sunlight there, spangling the water.

sand mandala. . .
the journey inward
until the wind

Nanuq

Curled inside the polar night, the white bear sleeps in a shallow well
of snow. Her back to the keening wind, paw a soft pillow. In a broken
swath of white, now smudged by the long dark, the bear embodies the field,
and the field the dreaming bear, dreaming a sheath of ice that extends
beyond the frame of her ken, dreaming she'll waken to swim through
her ancestry, out to a platform of years-old ice.

The ice will remember her immensity and the hunt. Ringed seals will rise
between thick floes. She is, after all, *Ursus maritimus*, the great white bear,
belonging to the land of the Shaman. Her spirit will return dressed as fur,
as shadow, as vapor. For now, her dream suspends the thaw, rafts into mine.

fog horn echo
the coast lost
in mist

Crosscurrent

The day is mild, only a slight breeze at our backs as my friend and I kayak
in Tarpon Bay, off Sanibel Island. We make our way through mangrove forest,
a twisting series of tunnels that eventually open out to ocean.

> *tenting. . .*
> *branches shadow*
> *the green dome*

The same gentle wind gathers strength as we turn our boats toward shore.
It muscles me out to open water. I dig in with my paddle just to remain in place.
My friend makes it to shore, calls to me, but the distance between us only
grows as my strength diminishes. Truly panicked, I feel myself giving in.

> *red flag*
> *water drains around the fish*
> *in the pelican's pouch*

A team of dolphins appears, flanks my kayak, swimming close, helping me
move forward. Are they cutting the headwind, making the current more favorable?
Or is their presence enough to urge me on.

Once on land, I turn to see the dolphins, but they have vanished just as suddenly
as they'd appeared.

comb jellies adrift
in the night lagoon
fairy lights

Note: collaborative haibun with prose by Barbara Sabol and haiku by *Marion Starling Boyer*

Crossing the Threshold

The old Cambria Public Library was my haven—floor to ceiling rows
of books with the promise of elsewhere bound in their weathered spines.

My cousin and I would spend whole afternoons in the alcoves,
drawn into new adventures—the ocean's depths, mountain jungles.
Unsupervised, yet silent and still as the wooden chairs we sat in.

branches cast
as shadow puppets
on the window shade

Something about the heady blend of aged paper and Pine Sol in that shushed
atmosphere tapped a new reverence in us. Different from being in church.
More like the woods at dusk when nymphs would come down from the trees.

                mom's third call
            to supper
        paddling
    my raft back
  to shore

Quarry

hideaway
in the attic eaves
reading *Lolita*

The old quarry-turned-swimming hole was an oasis on hot southern afternoons.
My girlfriends and I bushwhacked through the thick brush of ungroomed woods,
a good two miles in. Then we'd come upon it, a crater-sized bowl filled with bottle-
green water the texture of wet velvet. The temperature like cooled bathwater.
A sharp mineral scent swamped our senses.

Young women with unabashed bodies, we'd strip down to skin and cannonball
into the cool slur. Our glee echoed in the piney air. No doubt the quarry was also
a haven for cold-blooded life. The idea of swimming with a smartly banded snake
only added to the dangerous thrill.

    twig snap
        from behind a tree . . .
              the long lens

In Wait

As a child, I perfected the leap from threshold
to bed, clearing the space where the dreaded
monkey hands might reach up, grab an ankle,
drag me to a place darker than night. Even now,
I make a small hop into bed. Quick to slide my feet
beneath the covers.

swimming
in the shallows
a curved dorsal fin

Flare

through wavy
bonfire light
a blur of summer

As the weather turns cooler our crab apple burns
deeper in amber and auburn tones. Its small red
berries are match heads in the branches. A sunset
netted in our yard.

Gathering clouds of starlings swing from branch
to feeder, preparing for their long journey. Testing
the air, the invisible draw. Raucous, they announce
my own unspoken urge for somewhere else.

The blaze in our little square of earth is extinguished
in the first cold gust. A swift, easy release. And now
we rustle the leaves into parched mounds, then lean
on our rakes, watch the remains of the season blow
back in the chill wind.

torch song
the sawing of toothed wing
against wing

Given Back

The sun pale this late autumn afternoon, as though filtered
through gauze. Tea-stained tints of meadow grass and sedge
border the path. Now and then, I run my fingers through rushes,
silky as a child's hair. The land has been given back to itself—
returned to its instinctive sprawl, its mossy, hummocked earth,
its vernal pools. Winterberries in the low shrubs, cardinals
dotting the sycamores—vivid against this faded autumn palette.

century home wallpaper
under the heirloom roses
more roses

The sharp-toothed gears of the wetland have paused. Its industry now
is shelter—the pond snail burrows into soft earth, closes her door
to the coming cold; garter snakes twine in their hibernaculum. Still,
dormant life hums under my tread, like a promise. Nothing, nothing
but nature fanning out, digging in, cycling into what comes next.

snow-bound frog and i suspend the heart's rhythm

Why Our Mothers Warned Us About Playing in the Creek

It was less about jagged tin lids, or the mossy slickness of rocks
tumbled down from the hillside than bigger dangers our mothers
couldn't name. More about what was hatching beneath those rocks.
A quickening. Larvae set to emerge as nimble-legged, winged creatures.
The instinct to course into larger bodies of water. Or vanish into air.

that first puff
of a cigarette. . .
fading contrails

In the Wound of Night

—after Constantin Brâncuşi's sculpture, *Sleeping Muse*

I envy her perfection. More than beauty, her tranquility,
like a level's bubble, centered, even in this busy, brightly lit
gallery. A dream blooms inside the elegant head, at rest
on a pedestal. Cast in white marble, an ageless patina smooths
brow and cheek. The air around her shapes itself into clean,
linear features—an abstraction of woman, one you might know
at midnight; an evocation in the morning.

moon flower—
the night garden
fragrant with light

Tonight, in my ink dark bedroom, I imagine her crescent cheek
cradled on the pillow next to mine. Her mouth is inscrutable.
The marble softens at the Cupid's bow, allowing only the slightest
parting of her lips. I taste her cool breath as she descends into the deep
end of sleep; into a pool of lassitude.

A smile plays at the corners of her mouth. Her dreams must be
sweet, and so magically elsewhere. Lapis skies swirl with gold stars.
Exotic forests with sated tigers. I, too, close my eyes but my dreams
tousle out in the hall of my childhood home where people move
through dim rooms. There, no one has ever died. Everything
and nothing changed.

the ceiling fan's
rhythmic pulse—
missyou missyou missyou

Endangered

There is only one known
Peruvian village remaining
where a rope bridge is
stretched, peak-to-peak,
across a deep river gorge
in the Andes. Before
the prior year's bridge
collapses, the whole
community, children
to elders, works together
to construct a new bridge.
Women harvest straw grass,
and after the men hammer
it soft, the women and
children braid and bundle
the dried grass. The men
then weave the thick braids
into a bridge floor and rails,
suspend it above the river.
Ninety feet across. Safe
crossing hinges on flawless
work and many hands.
The Bridge Master says,
"We must care for the bridge.
We must adore it."

evening prayer—
swish of a puma's tail
behind the eucalyptus

To Whispering Cave

Some tired argument winds with us along the trail,
eclipsing birdsong, breeze, the tang of pine.

Around the next curve, a tower of Blackhand sandstone
rises from deep within the gorge. Silenced, we are lifted
out of ourselves.

rustle in the brush. . .
the white tag
of a solitary fox

Moist air from the ancient rock slakes our tongues.
A cool mineral bloom. Ocean once filled this place.
Above us, hemlock and yew reach, right angled
to the ledge. Roots tether the bedrock wall.

Now the late sun cuts across layers of stone and all this
needled greenness. Further on, the sudden rush of falls.

catch pool—
we ripple
and merge

Traveler

On our nightly walks, my dog will crane toward the occasional passing car, studying each driver's face, maybe searching for his first master, the one who might have taught him to lean full-bodied into love, who conditioned in him a fierce loyalty. Rescued from the street two counties away, my cherished companion may believe, in the instinctive sensory wash of canine thinking, that ever since, his first master has been driving everywhere, looking for him.

identifying
the bird in flight
by heart

If one day some driver should stop, push open the passenger door, call my dog by a name that pricks up his ears, makes him shiver and whine with joy, I wonder if I could release his leash, let him leap into the car. Then, with a resolve hard as love, close the door behind him.

half-hitch
the current's
constant draw

Late Light

After hours of digging, planting, mulching, our soft, aging bodies
fold into themselves. We rinse the good scent of garden coating
nailbeds and pulse points where summer insects gather.

As day distills to twilight, we sink into either end of the couch.
Routines of the long-married: my novel, the evening news until
a small strobe of light pulses in the corner of the room.

I set my book aside as one, no, two! fireflies cast their want
back and forth. The evening's mystery has followed us inside,
flashing its lonely code.

You pursue them, cupping one then the other in your palms.
How ordinary they look, small brown beetles, until they gather
their glow, making a lantern of your folded hands.

You elbow open the screen door, fling them out into the dark.
We watch as they *blink blink* desire into the night sky.

restless
in the bedroom's brightness
I slip to the yard
searching for a way
to forgive the moon

In the Garden I Am Reminded

The hydrangeas flower into October—blushing globes bud out
as the older, heavy-headed clusters drowse in the waning heat.
A fresh bouquet on the table each week. Buffer to the hard sorrows
of our black and white world. We must begin by believing beauty,
like goodness, persists.

Deep beneath the droughted earth rivers run cold and clean.
Old loves glimmer on, like planets of remote galaxies.
Next spring, seeds will rattle in their dried pods—a hint
of inflorescence just below the melting snow.

perpetual whirl—
the nautilus echoes
its fossil shell

Passing By

—to Martha, the last passenger pigeon

Easy prey, your kind. I imagine a massive brace of birds dimming
the daylight—thousands shaped as iridescent cloud, as specter.
The air must have vibrated with your *kee-kee-kee,* your mating bells.
I wish I could have stood, stock-still with the crowd, staring up,
astonished by your communal wheeling from tree to sky, sky
to roost, to sky again. Hunters need only have pointed their rifles
skyward.

Captured and caged when your numbers were reduced to three,
then two. A metal roof your sky. After your mate died, only you
on display at the Cincinnati Zoo. I like to think, after your 29 years,
you joined your flock on the other side of the sky in wild and endless
flight.

> plotting
> the next turn
> of the wheel—
> ashes mixed
> in sapling soil

Letting the Kneeler Down

Forgive me the absence of all feeling. My heart a pink spike.
I am a disposable animal, in exile from heaven. A bitter thing.
You must see I am attached to earth's delights—dark red petals,
sap frothing and rising. Distant father, are you stirred also?
I see beauty on either side of heaven: here, a yellow bird;
there, pleated wings, white fire.

Unreachable father, could you possibly exist? Lies have passed
between us like tiny aphids on the trailing rose. And silence.
If I say I love you, will you lift the weight of solitude? I speak
to you on my knees, my hands an empty clump of longing.

        after evening rain
        dark birds fold their wings

—cento sourced from the eight "Matins" poems from *The Wild Iris* by Louise Glück

Anticipation

—after William Carlos Williams

There are no chickens in the yard and it's snowing.
The wheelbarrow's red paint umber with rust. It leans
against the garden shed, slowly turning white. So much
depends on its winter vigil, its allegiance to spring.

strawberry moon gathering an early harvest

Ode to Spring, Peeper

After your frozen sleep, dreams of beetles, of robin song, of mud-sweet air,
of what passes for love at the wetland's edge, your heart resumes its lusty
rhythm, and you rustle awake in your snug of last autumn's leaves.

Small as a child's thumb, piercing as a night train, you stir the woods back to
what you sing for—another spring. So begins the forest song. Elsewhere, ice caps
weep into the sea; waters warm and rise. Yet here, this enormous chorus, a
hallelujah of miniature bells, beckons me out to the moon-struck yard.

long fallow. . .
sunflowers blaze all the way
to the skyline

Luck Is Luck

I turn my blessings like photographs into the light;
over my shoulder the god of Not-Yet looks on.
　　　　　　　　　　　—Jane Hirshfield

Hiking a gorge trail, I tripped, tumbled, landed hard. I lay there a long moment, my head spinning. Ankles, knees, elbows sore but in working order. Looking up through the branches at the cloudless sky, I gave thanks to the *god of not-yet*, who seems to follow me everywhere. Thank god, I whispered to the trees, thank god.

Chance, like a change in the weather, turns. So often out of the blue. I think of the stray rescued from a Russian street who spent one joyful day playing with the cosmonaut's children, and the next was blasted into space. They named her Laika—so close to Lucky.

shooting star
the impartial archer
draws his bow

Willingly

If the last sound I hear is a whir of sparrows, an all-at-once ascent from the apple tree, air pulsing above the branches, it would be a kind of permission. Like the luff of a sheet flung above the bed, again and again. That great whoosh of air takes me far out on the water, the sail breathing in and out. Coastline fading like memory.

immense heaven
feeling the tug
of other galaxies

Light sifts through the blinds tonight the way my mother sifted cake flour into a blue porcelain bowl. A dusting of twilight now on the chair, across the vanity. In her last days my mother swore she saw wings on the wall of her hospice room. First, it was a large bird. Later, an airplane. *Look*, she would say, hoisting herself up on her elbows, *can't you see the wings there on the wall*? Not a shadow of wings, but the wings themselves. She was insistent. *It's just the light playing tricks, Mom.* What else could I say?

But I'll admit that sometimes I can see the moon fall across the water, even though I live inland from the shore. I hear its swash, the riffle of beach pebbles. A commotion of gulls.

glass lake
trailing my fingers
through the clouds

Jigsaw

Through the brush I try to identify a bird whose body
is segmented by reeds and long-needled sugar pines—
puzzle-pieced. I first see a bar-striped wing, then the tip
of a down-curving beak. Next, its quick dip into marsh
water. A pencil-thin, yellow leg lifts, and now just toes
appear, splayed like a wrinkled rake. A flash of iridescent
green, stalking some elusive prey.

catching
her every other word—
static on the line

To the Neighborhood Coyote

The neighbors whisper, *menace, bandit*. Have they held your gaze?
Glimpsed your rough coat in the brush? I've been warned to avoid
that end of the block where brambles and rotting logs reclaim the land.

new moon shadow shape shifts

At night, your low-slung presence troubles the air. It's then
I am drawn to the hemmed-in mystery behind the rusted chain links.
Imagine a feral breath on my neck.

false alarm
the siren fades
to a whine

Lately, it's all I can do to keep from peering over the fence,
slipping it, risking the briars jutting through. Are you there,
crouched among the high weeds? And if I find you, what then?

face to face the desilvering mirror

hemlock trail . . .
we speak
in green

Animalia

A lioness leaps into the embrace of a beloved human; a crow brings offerings of tinsel and soda can tabs; a humpback protects a diver from a tiger shark by tucking her under its pectoral fin. I am envious of people who have crossed the boundary between human and wild life, that line between our quotidian lives and the realm inhabited by wild animals—a kingdom that fascinates, mystifies, thrills, and sometimes terrifies us. I believe the desire for bonding, if even briefly, with wild animals is a collective one. Witness how, as adults, we continue to be charmed by fairy tale animals. Imagine being invited to join the wise old Badger from *The Wind in the Willows* for a cup of tea and biscuits in his cozy den.

If we could step through the passageway into the realm of a furry, finned, or winged otherness, would the mystery of that creature persist? Would we step back somehow changed—wiser, fiercer? I believe that gaining entry to the world of the wild is a rare and privileged experience. It draws us from our solitary state and connects us to our own animal nature; our own wildness where our reflexes and sensory awareness are acute, where we know our range, exactly where we belong.

What then becomes of our instinctive nature when we restrict animals' ranges, even for their own protection; when large animals live within park boundaries, in zoos? Even worse, when animals are commodified, forced to live their least-best lives—dolphins in marine parks, gaudily clad circus elephants, canned big game hunts, monkeys in research labs. Are we taming the definition of "wild" and, by extension, "wilderness" when we exploit and "manage" animal life, when habitats are wiped out through deforestation? How then are own spirits damaged, our dreams of personal freedom and self-determination dulled?

When I was a child, my family visited the Brooklyn Zoo. This would have been in the early sixties before zoos began designing more expansive enclosures that mimic natural environments. I remember seeing a small wild cat, about the size of a lynx, in a cage only slightly larger than the animal. I watched as it frantically turned circles inside the small crate. Its desperation moved me to approach a guard, asking if he could find the animal a bigger cage. The man just smiled. During that same visit, there was a gorilla in a large, totally bare, brightly lit cage which was situated in a pit so that we could observe "the jungle beast" from above. He sat on a bench, the only object in that space, elbows on his knees, his head down. The posture of despair. Even at a young age, it was clear to me that he was depressed. My own spirit felt compressed, diminished, as well. The distinct memory of both those animals still haunts me.

While I am aware of the positive side of modern zoos—natural habitats, conservation, species preservation—I still resist visiting them. The pane of glass between me and a giraffe is a clear reminder that that magnificent animal is owned, monitored, controlled. Once when I visited a friend in Oregon, I had an afternoon to myself and chose to hike a trail in the Cascades known for cougar sightings. The stories and warnings were borne out by the sign posted at the trailhead which read *Hike at your own risk: cougar territory*. I wanted to lock eyes with a cougar, to come *this close*. At the same time, a low-level electric current ran through me; a mix of panic and excitement. I felt the big cat's eyes tracking my every step. Imagination overload or genuine intuition? I'll never know. The thrill of a possible sighting outweighed my common sense. But sitting in the safety of my living room watching a show about cougars could never match being in range of the real thing.

Another time, on a vacation in Georgia one May, a friend and I paddled the Okefenokee swamp, unaware that it was alligator mating season. The tannin-stained water obscured any movement below the surface. The bull gators' guttural roars echoed through the swamp, and frequent tail slaps signaled that an alligator had slid from the bank into and under the dark water. We gingerly dipped our oars through the blackwater channels, aware that an alligator might be beside or even beneath our canoe. Instead of fearing for my life, I felt fully—indeed, rapturously—alive.

Both adventures could be described as foolhardy, but isn't one pinch of foolishness and another of risk implicit in the idea of adventure? The impulse to explore the space inhabited by wild creatures isn't necessarily a death wish but is without doubt dangerous. That risk greatly increases when people venture well beyond natural boundaries and insert themselves into the lives and territory of wild animals. Consider Grizzly Man, who chose to live among the Alaskan grizzlies, trying to pet them, frolicking with their cubs. He was killed by the same bear he considered his kindred. Consider the "tourons" who attempt selfies with bison in the national parks. Consider Roy Horn of Siegfried and Roy whose 400-pound Siberian tiger went for his trainer's jugular on a stage in Las Vegas. These examples beg the question of just how far into a wild animal's kingdom we dare enter.

I believe that the allure of animal life is conditioned by more than the possible thrill of a wild encounter. There is a deep-seated identification with wildness, with what lives by instinct, an inborn cunning, a physical adroitness designed for self- and species preservation. A longing for oneness with the forest itself. Our civilized, tech-heavy lives with their ever-multiplying distractions and responsibilities have bred the lion's share of that primal savvy out of us. Perhaps we want to reclaim the sharpened sensory skills critical to our early ancestors' survival. More than a survival impulse is a longing to unravel the mysteries embodied by the animal kingdom: the salmon's return to its natal stream; the tern's thousand-mile migration across continents to the same nesting spot; the octopus's camouflage within a coral reef; the bees' patterned dance to communicate the location of nectar; the cicada whose internal calendar is marked for every 13th or 17th year. For every wild species there is a unique talent, a mystery.

There is a saying credited to the Nez Perce: "Every animal knows more than you do." We marvel, theorize, get at partial truths, but can we ever *know* in the bone-deep, selectively acquired knowing of animals? The larger question is whether we can really know our true nature, lighten the weight of our singular loneliness, absent a connection with the natural world. Animals manifest our core natural being, and bring us face-to-face with our native wildness, our life force, our wilderness.

In a recurring dream that I've had my whole adult life, I am walking a trail that runs alongside a clear stream. The scene is fully animated: trees are varied shades of green, shafts of light angle through the canopy, the water softly plashes over rocks in the stream, the air is cool. I am utterly at my ease; at peace. While aware that there are animals in these woods, I have no fear whatsoever. Then there comes a moment in the dream when I realize that this is the same path I've been trying to find again and again, one I walked as a child, and I am flooded with happiness. It is always at this moment that I wake up. The fulfillment found in the dream is replaced by a visceral need to find that trail; a longing to relive that experience of wholeness and rightness: senses fully engaged, at home in my body, being exactly where I belong.

Sheila-Na-Gig Editions

www.ingramcontent.com/pod-product-compliance
Lightning Source LLC
Chambersburg PA
CBHW081347120626
46546CB00011B/3478